To help the young soul,
to add energy,
inspire hope,
and blow the coals
into a useful flame;
to redeem defeat
by new thought and firm action,
this, though not easy,
is the work of divine man.

Ralph Waldo Emerson

To order additional copies of this handbook, or for information on
other WALK THE TALK® products and services,
contact us at
1.888.822.9255
or visit
www.walkthetalk.com

Inspired To Succeed

Printed in the United States of America
at MultiAd Inc.

$12.95
ISBN 978-1-885228-92-5

Contents

To Jeannette, Ryan and Connor
who inspire me each day
with what it means
to be a family

One small act. One massive impact.

In Talmud Yerushalmi, a sacred Jewish text, it reads, "I myself found fully grown carob trees in the world; as my fathers planted for me before I was born so do I plant for those who will come after me." In other words, the bounty that I enjoy now is because those before me planted what I now harvest – and so my obligation is to do the same for those who come next.

Generosity is the seed of legacy. We can inspire those we never meet because our actions speak for us.

Hilde Back never imagined the difference her act of generosity would have on so many lives. No doubt she hoped that by sponsoring Chris Mburu she could make a difference in his life – and so she did. But the fruits of her action multiplied when Chris took that gift of education and turned it into meteoric success. Rising from a poverty-stricken life in Kenya to the halls of Harvard University and eventually the United Nations, Chris exemplified the heights to which it is possible to soar if only we are given a chance.

There is no resume for greatness, no curriculum vitae for champions. Success does not insist on a pedigree. But to unleash one's potential does require an opportunity – and that is the gift that Hilde gave Chris.

But the gift kept on growing. Like ripples on a pond, what started with a few dollars a month from one retired Swedish teacher spread to become an international organization bearing her name that now sponsors hundreds of children. A bundle of grass no matter how dry cannot start a fire without a spark – opportunity is that spark that can ignite unimagined success.

When we take time to mentor those on our team, we are offering them an opportunity to excel. As leaders, investing our time with those who look to us for guidance is how we "sponsor" the next success story. The impact we have on developing leadership skills in our teammates ripples out as they grow and rise through the ranks. Our legacy as a leader is written years after we leave the stage in the actions of those we mentored.

Leaders aren't always tall, strong, powerful, prominent figures who dominate the room or command your attention. Sometimes, they are quaint, quiet, gentle souls who are no more conspicuous than a retired teacher. If leadership is inspiring others to rise above adversity and make a difference, then Hilde Back is a natural leader. She believed in the power of education to inspire young minds and knew that even one child was worth saving.

The teacher who opened the minds of thousands of children in her career discovered that her brightest pupil was one she never had in class.

Mother Teresa stated, "If you can't feed a hundred people, then just feed one." Hilde fed one mind and it changed the course of history in one African nation. Hilde was a victim of racism and genocide; Chris is a lawyer who fights those twin evils. Hilde was an educator; he shared her gift of education. Although they were a generation apart, their stories are inseparable.

Interwoven into the fabric of one leader's action are often the threads of other people's work. Our job as leaders is to see the tapestry for what it is – a diverse mosaic bound together by the hands of those who share a common belief. We all can make a difference but it starts with having an opportunity.

Who needs you to be their opportunity today?

How far that
little candle
throws his beams.
So shines a good deed
in a weary world.

William Shakespeare

Insight 2: Final Respects

My dad was the youngest of eight children – first-generation immigrants who were dirt-poor in money but rich in values. His dad died when he was six months old, and most of his siblings never made it to college or out of their rural Ohio roots. But his skill on the football field would take my dad to higher places, giving him a college education with a football scholarship and a lifelong passion for the game.

He died in 1995 at the age of 56. A retired Army officer and Bronze Star-decorated Vietnam veteran, he spent the last years of his life working as a civil engineer in Radcliff, Kentucky, just south of Louisville. In his spare time, Dad was an active high school football booster, eventually serving as the club's president. He took pride in building that organization into a model of charity and achievement.

His crown jewel as president was designing, funding and overseeing construction of the Power-House – a spectacular weight training facility on the high school campus that served to develop athleticism and strength in countless student-athletes. The Power-House is still there today, and a plaque on the wall celebrates the contribution my dad made to its construction. But beyond the bricks and mortar, Dad cared about the players.

Dad was always a leader, a mentor and something of a magnet to players who flocked to him for insight, stories or a good word. Long after his own sons had played and graduated, Dad stayed active in the high school football program, and so year after year players knew him on sight.

Indeed, many times a player would approach him after practice or a game and say, "Mr. Novak, can I ask you something?" And off they would walk.

When Dad died, the community wept. Hundreds turned out for his calling hours. The line of people paying their respects was humbling, but one moment stands out quite vividly for me.

Dad's casket was in a large open room with dozens of chairs off to the back for people to sit and reflect – and many did. But there was one young man in his early twenties who caught my eye as he sat, head in his hands, in the very back corner of the room. I noticed him because he stayed the entire time – even the extra hours that had to be added to get all of the people through the receiving line. He stayed there as others came and went. When the front door to the funeral home finally was closed and calling hours were finished, my family gathered in another room to rest and talk.

I happened to drift back into the viewing room; as I came to the entrance I stopped. There, on the far side of the room, the young man who had sat for hours in the back was kneeling at Dad's casket shedding a torrent of tears. I stood motionless and silent, not wanting to disturb this intensely personal and painful moment. I watched as he made the sign of the cross, stood up and turned to leave. We made eye contact, and as he stepped across the room I approached him. He expressed his condolences so I asked him how he knew my dad.

"From football," he paused, then continued. "He gave me something I really needed back then."

"What was that?" I asked.

"His time," he said.

He went on about my dad as a man the team loved not just for the Power-House they knew he had created but for the way he connected with players on a personal level.

15

"All the kids knew your dad and respected him a lot. He made time for all of us. He cared."

He shook my hand and turned to leave the room but stopped and turned back to face me.

"Your dad told me something once that I never forgot. I was walking with him out the stadium gate one night after a game that we had played our hearts out but lost," the young man said.

"Your dad saw how devastated I was, and he put his arm around my shoulder, looked me in the eyes and said, 'Son, someone has to lose the football game, but no one who plays their heart out ever leaves the field a loser.' I never forgot those words."

It turns out that the young man was now a junior in college. He had been talking with his parents the night before when they told him that Mr. Novak had passed away suddenly. The young man hung up the phone, climbed into his car and drove through the night from Michigan to Kentucky to be at the funeral home in time for calling hours – surprising even his parents when he arrived.

When they asked him what he was doing there, he told them he had to come to say goodbye to a man who had made a difference in his life.

Lessons For Leaders

My dad made a difference with nothing more than a few minutes and a few words offered from the heart to someone he knew only in passing but who needed him to care. But then, that's no surprise.

Leaders care about others not because they want something *from* them but because they have something *for* them.

Making a difference isn't *doing* something; it's *being* something – being available, being involved, being concerned, being proud, being patient, being honest or just being there.

I was facilitating a leadership training session recently and I asked the participants to think of the best leader they had ever worked for and what it was about that person that made such an impact. One of the defining characteristics was the leader's constant availability.

Time is the most valuable commodity we can offer as a leader – coaching, mentoring, praising and just caring about the people we lead outweigh giving raises, bonuses, stock options and perks. It takes discipline to not let the ring tones rule or not let the hours slip away to e-mail, inboxes or overbooked calendars, but we must find a balance. Leadership is not something we can phone in; it's a responsibility we exercise in person, face to face, every day.

At work, do not reward people with your absence – spend time with your high performers rather than assuming they want to be left alone. They don't. At home, immerse yourself in the abundance of life that takes only the will to be fully present to enjoy. Leave the laptop in its case, shut off the cell phone and rediscover home life.

Then find meaningful ways to give back. It isn't *what* you do that counts; it's *that* you do. Reach out beyond yourself to people you do not know, to people who could not possibly repay even an ounce of your kindness, and give back without hesitation. There is no such thing as a small kindness – every act is priceless.

The best leaders change us. They make us better. They move us in ways we don't always recognize at first but never forget.

Dad knew the power of leading with his heart; he lived it and he passed it on in a messenger who drove through the night to pay final respects for a single moment of caring that had a lifetime of impact.

Never give up,
for that is just the
place and time
that the tide will turn.

Harriet Beecher Stowe

Insight 3: Speaker's Choice

Inspiration often has humble beginnings.

Leslie Calvin Brown and his twin brother, Wesley, were born in 1945, on the floor of an abandoned building in Liberty City, a low-income section of Miami, Florida, to a mother who gave them up for adoption three weeks later. At six weeks of age, both boys were adopted by Mamie Brown, a 38-year-old single cafeteria cook and domestic worker who had small means but a big heart and an unfailing belief that there was greatness inside the boys.

For Les Brown, that greatness would be slow to emerge.

In school, Brown was a poor student because he was unable to concentrate, especially in reading. His restlessness and inattentiveness, coupled with his teachers' impatience, resulted in his being labeled "educably mentally retarded" in the fifth grade. It was a label he found hard to remove, in large part because he did not try.

"They said I was slow so I held to that pace," he recounted later in his book, *Live Your Dreams*.

But greatness is nurtured with great mentors.

LeRoy Washington, a speech and drama instructor at Booker T. Washington High School in Miami, would become a catalyst for inspiring Brown to discard that label and attitude. Brown once told Washington in class that he couldn't perform a task because he was educably mentally retarded. The instructor responded, "Do not ever say that again! Someone's opinion of you does not have to become your reality."

Those words would liberate Brown from his debilitating mindset.

"The limitations you have, and the negative
things that you internalize are given to you by the
world," he wrote of his realization. "The things
that empower you – the possibilities – come from
within."

Brown got a job as a garbage man after high school but his
determination to do more with his life ran high. He set his mind on a
career in radio broadcasting and pestered the owner of a local station
about a position until the owner hired him to sweep floors. He learned
all he could about the workings of a radio station. One day, when a
disc jockey was unable to work, Brown filled in at the microphone and
started a brilliant career in media that would include a top-rated radio
program in Columbus, Ohio.

Brown eventually ran for the Ohio State Legislature, winning the seat of
the 29th House District. In his first year, he passed more legislation than
any other freshman representative in Ohio legislative history. In his third
term, he served as chair of the Human Resources Committee.

He left state government in 1981 to care for his ailing mother in
Florida, but in walking away from politics, Brown walked into what
would become his signature life's work. It was a chance meeting with
motivational speaking icon, Zig Ziglar, that lit a fire in Les Brown that
had been smoldering all of his life.

Brown started his motivational speaking career with nothing, moving to
Detroit with just his clothes and one tape of his motivational speeches.
He rented an office that he literally never left – he slept on the floor

because he could not afford an apartment. Brown read books on public speaking and studied the habits of established speakers.

He first spoke to grade school students, then high school students. Clubs and organizations followed. Less than four years later, in 1989, he received the National Speakers Association's highest award, the Council of Peers Award of Excellence, becoming the first African American to receive such an honor. He was known in professional circles as "The Motivator."

In 1990, Brown recorded the first in a series of motivational speech presentations for the Public Broadcasting Service. He spoke not only to executives of corporations but also to prison inmates and, remembering his own background, to special education students in high schools.

"We all have a responsibility to give something back," he said. "I am who I am because of the relationships I have developed, because of the people who have enriched my life."

Through it all, his mission remained simple: to get a message out that will help people become uncomfortable with their mediocrity. He explained, "A lot of people are content with their discontent. I want to be a catalyst to enable them to see themselves having more and achieving more."

Lessons For Leaders

Les Brown saw his mission as helping people become uncomfortable with their mediocrity. It is a powerful aspect of leadership that often goes untested because it means confronting those who can do more and be more. It isn't just pushing the weak to become acceptable; it's often challenging the strong to be champions.

Mediocrity isn't being marginal; it's being stagnant.

Leadership does not suffer mediocrity well. It has no place for those who desire only to tread water and bob in their current circumstances. Leadership is about moving boldly in the direction of one's dreams and goals – even when those distant shores are not in view or the waters are filled with dangerous creatures. Leaders are never comfortable with the status quo; they are always in search of growth, change and continuous improvement. To a leader, stagnation is death-by-omission.

But how aggressive are we in addressing mediocrity in our ranks? As leaders, have we grown too comfortable with our own skills and expectations?

Mark Twain stated, "Keep away from those who try to belittle your ambitions. Small people always do that, but the really great make you believe that you too can become great."

Les Brown made people feel that they too had greatness inside. I know because he inspired me. Years before I would ever take the stage for a "Conquering Adversity" keynote, I marveled at and studied a man so passionate with his words.

Our responsibility as leaders is to help those we lead see the greatness they possess and then harness it for the team's benefit. What are we doing today to help those on our team see (and reach) their full potential?

Humility is its own greatness.

Here is a man who was given up at birth, labeled as mentally retarded, started his professional life as a garbage man, swept floors to get into radio, slept on a bare office floor to launch his speaking career and yet finds in himself a message to share with millions of people around the world about how they too can be great.

No beginning is so humble that it cannot contain the seeds of greatness.

Les Brown's journey and success are yet another inspiring example that the heights to which a person rises in life is not determined as much by where they came from as it is by where they are going.

So ask yourself, "Where are you going? Where is your team headed?"

My will shall shape the future.
Whether I fail or succeed
shall be no man's doing
but my own.
I am the force;
I can clear any obstacle
before me or
I can be lost in the maze.
My choice; my responsibility;
win or lose, only I hold the key
to my destiny.

Elaine Maxwell

Insight 4: Broken Better Than New

Eugene Maurice Orowitz, nicknamed "Emo," grew up a miserable boy in a dysfunctional family. His parents fought bitterly. His father's career as a movie publicist crumbled. His mother, a former actress, was suicidal. He was a skinny, angry, half-Catholic, half-Jewish kid with a genius IQ who struggled in school under merciless taunts. Adding to his grief, he was a late bedwetter whose mother humiliated him by hanging his wet sheets out the window of his Collingswood, New Jersey, home for all to see.

It was not a pedigree for greatness – but then, greatness is summoned up, not handed down.

One day in high school, Eugene's physical education teacher took the class out to the football field to teach them to throw a javelin. One by one, the boys stepped up, took hold of the menacing projectile and hurled it out across the field – ten yards for some, twenty yards for others and even thirty yards.

Last in line was Eugene. A chorus of taunts rained down on the boy … "Don't hurt yourself, Emo!" … "Try not to drop it, you weakling!" … and worse.

But the teacher silenced them all and walked up to a tight-lipped Eugene who was already shaking his head "no" to throwing in front of his tormentors. The teacher insisted, and with the javelin extended and a few encouraging words, he invited the young boy to try.

Eugene grasped the javelin, looked downfield, glanced at the boys who were still mocking him with their faces and gestures, and then taking six rapid steps he sent the javelin airborne – ten yards, twenty yards, thirty yards … forty yards … fifty yards … sixty yards!

The javelin crashed into the empty stadium seats beyond the end zone, having gone twice as far as any of the other boys who stood in silent awe at the spectacle they had just witnessed. Eugene could throw a javelin!

When the teacher retrieved the javelin, the tip was broken from the stadium impact, so he offered the pieces to Eugene who repaired the lance and began practicing with it in earnest.

Together, that once-broken javelin and that once-broken boy began a surprising journey that would touch the heart of a nation.

But not in the way you are thinking.

You see, while it is true that Eugene practiced throughout high school at throwing the javelin and became extremely good at it – so good, in fact, that he earned a full athletic scholarship to UCLA and moved west to pursue his dream of Olympic gold – this is not a story about track and field glory.

In fact, it's about a failure that Eugene would later say was one of the best things that ever happened to him.

Early in his freshman year at UCLA, Eugene was throwing the javelin without having properly warmed up and he tore the ligaments in his shoulder. The injury was so severe that he could not throw a javelin ever again and so UCLA withdrew his scholarship. Eugene had to quit school and took a series of manual labor jobs to make ends meet.

Adrift, Eugene had no real direction in life until he agreed to help a friend audition for Warner Brothers' acting school. In an ironic twist of fate, the friend didn't get the job but Eugene did, launching a career in film and television that would eventually span nearly four decades.

Eugene was so successful in television that to this day no other actor has ever had three back-to-back dramatic series spanning a longer time period (1959–1989) than he did. His work was so compelling that over those 30 years on the small screen, he morphed for millions of Americans from the quintessential son into the sage father and finally into a heavenly Godsend.

The boy who threw the javelin into the seats that day would later get a standing ovation on Johnny Carson's *The Tonight Show* as he bid the country farewell just a few months before pancreatic cancer took his life at age 54.

Eugene Maurice Orowitz is today an icon of American television where generations came to love him as *Bonanza's* "Little Joe" Cartwright, *Little House on the Prairie's* Charles Ingalls and *Highway to Heaven's* Jonathan Smith.

Millions knew him better by a stage name he chose out of a phone book, Michael Landon.

Lessons For Leaders

There is no pedigree for greatness, no resume for excellence, no CV for fortitude. What we are is what we summon from within when what we expect is no more. Leadership of self always precedes leadership of others.

Michael Landon's journey from a depressed, angry bedwetting boy to an iconic television hero is a vivid reminder that we measure people not by where they start but by how they finish. Self-leadership means the courage to face your fears and your critics – to step up, grab hold and hurl yourself forward even when the outcome is uncertain.

The path of least resistance would have been to refuse the teacher's invitation to try the javelin, accept the taunts that came anyway and slip to the back of the line. But something deep inside gave young Orowitz just enough defiance to try – and in that one throw, change the course of his life and others'.

It had to be a magical moment. Eugene had never even held a javelin before so throwing one twice as far as anyone else that day had to feel incredible.

It is empowering to discover something we have a special talent for – especially when we didn't know it was a special talent. Self-leadership begins with self-discovery and that is a journey with many guides.

A teacher who would not take "no" for an answer when it was Eugene's turn to throw became the catalyst for a career not even imagined yet.

Indeed, in discovering that one talent – the javelin throw – Eugene Orowitz would eventually find his true passion in life – acting. It was a revelation inspired not by fulfilling his dream of Olympic gold but by failing to ever reach it.

The pursuit of one dream put him on the path to achieve another.

Leaders know that failure carries more opportunity than finality if you are willing to push through the adversity – a career-ending injury becomes a career-launching break.

Leading ourselves is more challenging than leading others. But it is a prerequisite. We are not effective team leaders if first we are not effective self-leaders. Until we are tested, we cannot know the depth of our abilities or the strength of our character. Rather than fearing such discovery, leaders embrace it for the opportunity it offers.

Finally, beyond our own journey, we must be the teacher who does not take "no" for an answer. As leaders, we are the voice that must silence the do-nothing critics while encouraging the hesitant to reach past what was once broken and discover the hero that waits inside each of us.

I've seen and met angels
wearing the disguise
of ordinary people
living ordinary lives.

Tracy Chapman

Insight 5: Winton's Children

The year was 1938 and the winds of war were gathering over an uneasy Europe. A 30-year-old clerk at the London Stock Exchange, Nicholas Winton, accepted an invitation from a friend at the British Embassy in Prague, Czechoslovakia, to visit. While there, he lent a hand in the newly built refugee camps that were filling up with thousands of Czech families fleeing the imminent Nazi invasion. The young Englishman was moved by the tremendous need to do something for the children in these camps, and so he decided to do whatever was in his power to put the children outside the reach of the Nazi regime.

Working from the dining room table of his hotel room in Prague, Nicholas set up an organization that would send children to host families in Britain. Word spread of his efforts. Desperate parents flocked to the hotel to put their children's names on a list Nicholas created to be transported to London.

"It seemed hopeless," Nicholas would say years later in reflecting on how difficult it was to determine whose situation was most urgent. But he knew he had to save as many as he could before war broke out, so Nicholas left Prague in early 1939 to make arrangements in Britain for the children's arrival and adoptions.

Back in London, Nicholas worked with the British Committee for Refugees from Czechoslovakia on getting the children out. Tireless in his efforts, he finally persuaded Britain's Home Office to let the children in, but for each child he had to find a foster parent and have a 50 pound guarantee, a small fortune in those days. He also had to raise money to help pay for the transports when contributions by the children's parents couldn't cover the costs. He did all this practically on his own and after working his day job as a clerk.

Over the next several months, he arranged eight trainloads carrying a total of 669 children to travel from Prague to London. He met every train and watched 669 exhausted children, with name tags draped around their neck, walk off the railcars and into the arms of waiting English families.

A ninth train with 250 children was set to leave on September 3, 1939, but on that date Britain entered the war and the border was closed. None of the 250 children onboard was seen again, and the ensuing holocaust claimed more than 15,000 Czech children. It was an unimaginable tragedy but mercifully not for 669 children whose miracle came in the guise of an English clerk.

Nicholas Winton spoke very little about his role saving those children. It wasn't his way. For 50 years almost no one, not even his wife, knew what he had accomplished.

Then, in 1988, his wife found dusty boxes containing Nicholas' old documents, log books and the lists of children he had saved. His heroism was rediscovered.

Every child saved was special. One of the 669 children would grow up to be a Lord in the British Parliament; another was a cousin of Czech-born and former U.S. Secretary of State Madeleine Albright; one became a famous film director, another a respected author, another an Israeli pilot and so on.

In 2001, at the invitation of Czech President Vaclav Havel, Nicholas returned to Prague along with about 250 of the 669 children, now grown and many of them grandparents, to view the premier of a film about his story titled *Nicholas Winton – the Power of Good.* The film would win an International Emmy Award in 2002. Survivors, who call themselves "Winton's children," relished the opportunity to thank the man who had saved their lives.

In 2002, he was knighted by the Queen of England. In 2007, Sir Nicholas Winton received the Czech Republic's highest military honor, the *Cross of the 1st Class.* In that same year, schoolchildren across the Czech Republic collected tens of thousands of signatures to submit his name for the Nobel Peace Prize.

Now more than 100 years old and still impeccably humble, Nicholas dismisses his designation as the Schindler of Britain, insisting that he wasn't anything special. "I just saw what was going on and did what I could to help."

Lessons For Leaders

Every opportunity to lead is important.

What we do as leaders makes a difference. The lives we impact matter. The actions we take have consequences that resonate far beyond the moment. While we may never face the magnitude of crisis that Nicholas Winton did, we should be mindful that leadership is not a "sometimes" thing.

There are no small leadership moments; every situation we engage changes something or someone.

Nicholas Winton did not go to Prague to save children. He did not go there to become a hero. He did not go looking for a moment to change history, but that moment found him and he answered. There were literally thousands of people similarly situated at that same place and time who could have done what Nicholas did and yet they did not act with the same bold leadership of this clerk. Why? What was it about Nicholas Winton that caused him to lead when others watched, to act when others waited?

First, he got involved. Others in Prague knew there were refugee camps, but Nicholas worked in them, volunteered to help and experienced the need firsthand. Leaders are not afraid to roll up their sleeves and do whatever work is required. They understand the issues because they become part of them, and that involvement helps to shape their opinions and guide their actions. They connect with the people closest to the need, and that bond serves as a catalyst to respond more urgently than someone on the outside looking in.

There is a time and place for objectivity and distance from an issue, but more often than not leaders who immerse themselves in the challenge make the high-impact decisions that matter.

Nicholas teaches us the elegance of humility. This was not a politician, a general, a CEO or any prominent person trained in leadership. Here was a simple man whose personal commitment to complete strangers resulted in hundreds of children being saved from a horrific fate, and yet he trumpeted none of his achievements. He kept the proof of his greatness tucked away in dusty boxes, with stories of the difference he made during the dark days of the war, silent from even his wife. He did not need accolades to validate his actions; he just did what he thought was right. That is what true leaders do. Leadership doesn't need a marketing campaign. It doesn't seek the limelight.

Leadership is an unyielding but quiet force of purposeful motion that moves mountains unseen in the night and leaves it for others to ponder in daylight who it was that accomplished so monumental a task.

What is it about your leadership efforts that people will find inspiring years from now? Leadership comes from the heart not the title. True leaders motivate the inside to drive the outside. The children whom Nicholas saved grew up and influenced other people; and like ripples on a pond, the actions of this one transformed many. Whose life did you make a difference in today?

"I just saw what was going on and did what I could to help," Nicholas said – so beautiful a definition of leadership from one of its most humble voices.

Do not let
what you cannot do
interfere with
what you can do.

Coach John Wooden

Insight 6: Class Act

I watched as my 1999 Mercedes ML320 was hauled away for scrap after being hit hard from behind and totaled. But despite 11 years of driving and over 140,000 miles, the "tank" protected its driver from deadly harm, and for that I was unimaginably grateful.

Ironically, as dramatic as its ending was, this story is about the vehicle's beginning.

My son, Ryan, was 9 years old in 1998 when his mom, Cynthia, seven months pregnant with our second child, was killed as she drove home from work by a man high on drugs who ran a stop sign at high speed. The nightmare devastated our lives. One of my earliest challenges after Cynthia's death was getting Ryan into a car – he was terrified we would be hit too. In his mind, he feared every intersection. It was heartbreaking.

To help him, I told Ryan that we would buy the safest car on the road. We would search out a vehicle that was a "tank" and made us both feel safe. The answer was a Mercedes ML320 sport utility vehicle, a new SUV at the time with all the right stuff to allay Ryan's fears. Our local Syracuse dealer, Romano Motors, had a website, and so a few weeks after the funeral I sent a lengthy email describing the tragedy, sharing Ryan's fears and the importance of this vehicle. Thankfully, the right person read it.

A few days later, I went to Romano's to test-drive the vehicle. I knew immediately it was exactly what Ryan and I had thought it would be – big, strong and safe. Back on the lot, I told the salesman that I wanted one. He laughed at me and explained that there was an 18-month waiting list for delivery of that model and no way to get one any sooner.

I was crushed and I knew Ryan would be crushed. Deflated, I said goodbye to the salesman who then asked me my name. When I told him, he stopped and said, "Come with me, please!"

I followed him into an empty general manager's office where I noticed a piece of paper on the desk. It was a printout of my email marked with highlighter and notes written up the margin.

The GM, Jim Poissant, came in and introduced himself. He told me how sorry he was about my wife's death. He said he could not imagine the pain of that experience and asked how Ryan was doing. I told him each day was still a struggle and that he was going to be so disappointed at the news that we couldn't get the ML320.

Jim looked me in the eyes and said, "We're not going to disappoint your son."

He told me that after he read my email he called Mercedes-Benz of North America and shared the story with some senior leaders there. He said they agreed that this was an extraordinary circumstance and that Mercedes-Benz would do whatever it took to help. Jim said the instruction he got from his corporate leadership was simple, "Find Mr. Novak, and if he wants this vehicle, we will build him one."

I was speechless. Jim smiled and then asked me quite nonchalantly, "So, would you like them to build one for you and your son?" "Yes," I replied. We shook hands and he said he would call me when the vehicle was ready.

Thirty days later, Mercedes-Benz delivered the vehicle – thirty days. Jim personally took Ryan on a tour of the new SUV, showing him every gadget, button and talking about how safe it was. I watched Ryan's face as fear was replaced with excitement, and I knew that we had turned one small corner in our long journey forward.

We traveled everywhere together in that car, racking up miles and memories. When Ryan was 16, he learned to drive in that car, and later, it was his wheels for his first two years of college.

The ML320 showed its age many times but there was never a thought to trade or sell it – no way. It was far too special.

Jim is still the GM at Romano Motors, and he was there when I retrieved a few things from the now totaled family relic. We reminisced and I thanked him again for caring enough all those years ago to make that purchase possible. He said it was nothing.

I told him he couldn't be more wrong.

Leaders value the unexpected opportunity. They not only see big moments, they create them. Leaders don't let current boundaries limit a team's potential to be extraordinary. As a leader, Jim Poissant understood that excellence flows not from doing what is expected but from what no one would expect.

Jim could easily have ignored my email as a sad story that he couldn't do anything about. He had plenty of sales; he had never met me and helping me meant going up the chain to create an exception. There was no obvious reason to act on my behalf. But the obvious is not what drives a leader. Instead, Jim saw it as a chance for his organization to shine.

Jim knew it wasn't about making the sale; it was about making a difference.

In sharing my story with senior leaders at Mercedes-Benz headquarters, Jim pushed the case that the company had a true opportunity to do something special. His advocacy brought the situation to the attention of top decision makers who agreed with Jim and supported his actions.

This wasn't one man striking out on his own to do something his organization opposed; it was one man offering his team a chance to unleash the best of what they already were – a class act.

And Mercedes-Benz responded – give an organization a chance to excel and the best always will.

On the P&L for Mercedes-Benz in 1998, the sale of one ML320 to a customer in Syracuse, New York, went completely unnoticed.

An obscure fraction of the tens of thousands of their employees knew that the company had built one very special SUV that year, and even they might have forgotten the act.

There was no publicity or fanfare for what they did; no marketing campaign drove their decision. They just did it quietly and without hesitation because that's who they were as individuals and as an organization.

But for a 9-year-old boy riding confidently in the passenger seat of his shiny new "tank," the sale was anything but insignificant. In fact, it was transformational.

Every mile took him a little farther away from a tragedy that had changed his life; every trip was filled with a little less fear and a little more hope.

Tell me what that means to a father, and you begin to get an idea of the importance of that one decision to go beyond what was expected to what was needed – and do it for someone they had never met.

Jim Poissant went the extra mile. Mercedes-Benz went the extra mile – not because they had to but because they wanted to, because it allowed them to demonstrate the very best that they purported to be.

Leadership means sometimes coloring outside the lines, bending a few "rules." Customers were waiting for Mercedes-Benz to build that vehicle, but they decided to push one order to the top of the list. No hesitation. No issues.

Doing more than what is expected is effort; doing what isn't expected is character; but doing it quietly in the life of a brokenhearted little boy is class.

Kindness is the language
which the deaf can hear
and the blind can see.

Mark Twain

Insight 7: Repaid in Kind

In the late nineteenth century a Member of the British Parliament was making a trip to Scotland for a speech. After traveling by train to Edinburgh, he took a carriage south toward his destination. But along an isolated stretch of Scottish countryside, the carriage became mired in the mud.

To the rescue came a Scottish farm boy named Alexander and his team of horses who, with some effort and persistence, pulled the stuck carriage free and set the gentleman on his way.

Grateful for the rescue, the dignitary asked the boy how much he owed him for his act of kindness.

"Nothing," replied the lad.

"Nothing, are you sure?" prodded the man.

"Yes, nothing," Alexander replied again.

Impressed with the young lad's graciousness, the Member of Parliament asked the boy, "Is there anything I can do for you? What do you want to do with yourself when you grow up?"

Without hesitation, the young lad answered back, "I want to be a doctor." It was a big dream for a boy living in the modest surroundings of Scottish farm life, but that was indeed what the boy desired most.

The man smiled and said, "Well, then let me help you do just that."

He directed Alexander to contact him when he was old enough to attend university, and he promised to help.

It was a promise the aristocratic Englishman kept, as years later the man sponsored Alexander's college education and watched the Scot graduate and become a doctor.

But the elder statesman could never have imagined how important keeping his promise to help the boy would be or how valuable that boy's chosen career path would become.

More than 50 years later and a continent away, one of the world's greatest statesmen lay dangerously close to death with pneumonia. Winston Churchill, attending a wartime conference in Morocco, had fallen gravely ill.

But a wonder drug was administered to him – a new medicine called penicillin – discovered by a Scottish doctor, Sir Alexander Fleming.

The same Alexander Fleming who had helped a stranger decades before along a road near his home in Scotland.

But this story has one more twist.

The stranger mired in the mud of the Scottish countryside that day was Randolph Churchill.

By keeping his promise to help the farm boy get an education as a doctor, Randolph Churchill set in motion a process that would lead to the discovery of the very drug that decades later saved the life of Randolph's son, Winston.

How far does kindness reach? Sometimes, across decades.

Life is a series of chain reactions. One act of kindness – helping a stranger stuck on the roadside – collides with another act of kindness – helping a young man attend university – and the result is a stream of events that saved the stranger's son and changed the world. Generosity sets in motion actions whose outcomes may be unseen for years but whose impact can be miraculous.

Are you strong enough to be kind?

Kindness isn't weakness; it's the strength of conviction to do the right thing simply because it is the right thing.

Kindness has no scale; it does not measure the worth of one gesture to another but rather finds momentum in the collective goodwill of all those engaged in producing its outcomes. Kindness is not a debt to be repaid; it is a partnership between the helped and the helper, a bond of common experience that inspires both to do more.

Kindness is need meeting means, with no one else around. Kindness does not create a debt; it offers an opportunity.

Will you seize that opportunity? Do you have the courage to demonstrate kindness?

As leaders, we need to be an example of kindness in action. We need to keep the promises we make. We need to recognize the people on our team who make a difference and not just thank them for that positive contribution but build on it with our own. Kindness is at the heart of the servant-leader. It debunks the notion that leadership wears a stone face or turns a blind eye or keeps a distance from people – leaders know the inspiration of generosity and the power of empathy to motivate a team.

We pass them every day at work, at home, in our community – people stuck along the roadside of life. Sometimes to help the lift is heavy; other times it needs just a kind word. But do we stop? Do we help? Do we ask anything in return? It is easy to be so caught up in our daily challenges that we miss the opportunities that surround us to make a difference in someone's life. It can be a colleague, a family member, a neighbor, a friend or a complete stranger – the only common denominator is a need for someone to care enough to act.

Charity is an act; kindness is a value. Both have merit but kindness understands that gratitude is a gesture, attitude is a statement. When we have an attitude that lives and leads with kindness, we leave a trail of goodwill in our wake that others can follow and build upon. Kindness is not what we say; it's what we do. You do not repay kindness; you replenish it.

Randolph Churchill saw Alexander Fleming's act of kindness as more than a stroke of good fortune that allowed him to attend a conference on time. He saw it as an opportunity to change a young man's life; what he didn't realize was it would also be the difference in saving his own son's life.

There are no limits to the impact of an act of kindness, no boundaries on its potential. Who can you help "out of the mud" today? How can you inspire your team to stop for the stranger? Lead with a kind heart and great things are always possible.

Aerodynamically
the bumblebee
shouldn't be able to fly,
but the bumblebee
doesn't know that
so it goes on flying anyway.

Mary Kay Ash

Insight 8: Square Peg in a Round Hole

"Houston, we have a problem."

Tom Hanks immortalized those words in the 1995 movie *Apollo 13,* and they have come to symbolize every unanticipated crisis that threatens to lead to catastrophe without immediate intervention – and for good reason. The problems NASA faced in 1970 in trying to save three astronauts trapped in a seriously disabled spacecraft were complex and unprecedented.

But one problem in particular threatened to doom the crew with literally every breath. Fortunately, a Southern gentleman with a brilliant mind and calm style brought a breath of fresh air to the crisis.

Robert "Ed" Smylie was born Christmas Day, 1929, on his grandfather's farm in Lincoln County, Mississippi. His father managed a local ice plant, and at an early age Smylie's mother made it clear that her son would make school a priority. He did, earning a bachelor's degree and a master's degree in mechanical engineering from Mississippi State University and a graduate degree in management from MIT.

After spending time in the armed forces and teaching, Smylie began his engineering career at Douglas Aircraft. NASA hired him in 1962, and seven years later his calm style helped him become acting chief of the crew systems unit – the team entrusted with keeping astronauts alive.

When an oxygen tank exploded on the way to the moon, *Apollo 13's* crew was forced to evacuate the larger service module and move into the tiny lunar module, which was designed for just two astronauts – not three. The extra burden overloaded the environmental control systems that filter out exhaled carbon dioxide. Without a sufficient filter, CO_2 levels would rise and the astronauts would choke to death two days before reaching earth re-entry. Compounding the problem, the filter systems of the service module and the lunar module were incompatible – NASA had to literally fit a square peg into a round hole.

"I was watching TV at home and when they broke into the program to say there was a problem with *Apollo 13,* I just drove out to the center. I only lived five minutes away," said Smylie.

Unlike the movie, workers at the Lyndon B. Johnson Space Center in Houston stayed cool in spite of the grave circumstances.

"Nobody raised a voice the entire time," he said. "If you did it the way it actually happened, you would have had a pretty dull movie."

But leaders don't need flash or sizzle, just results.

Smylie got a list of everything the astronauts had onboard the spacecraft and, not unlike the movie, he and his team dumped all of that material onto a table and set about figuring how they could turn paper, plastic, cardboard, socks, tubing and odds and ends into a filter capable of scrubbing the CO_2. Ed's biggest relief was learning that duct tape was onboard. (Problem-solving is always easier with duct tape.)

For six hours, Smylie's team built and tested a new filter using the materials available to the astronauts. "We jury-rigged a system where we used a plastic bag, cardboard off the flight plan and duct tape to connect those square canisters to the lunar module's (round) environment control system," Smylie said.

Joe Kerwin, an astronaut and designated *Apollo 13* capsule communicator, still remembers Smylie and his team walking into mission control and spreading out all of the gear in front of his console along with a checklist of instructions for him to give the astronauts to build the filter.

"Ed was probably the finest crew systems chief we had," said Kerwin. "He's very orderly, very methodical, and he does that in a way that garners the confidence of the people he's working with."

Within a half hour after the filter was installed, the carbon dioxide levels in the ship fell to normal.

Following the astronauts' safe return, President Richard Nixon presented Smylie and his team with the Presidential Medal of Freedom for solving the CO_2 crisis.

"Had that not occurred these men would not have gotten back," Nixon said. "That is only one example to prove the magnificent teamwork of the whole group."

Yes, one example of teamwork among many, but definitely one of those all-or-nothing moments for three astronauts who were suffocating one breath at a time a long, long way from home and in desperate need of a leadership miracle.

Lessons For Leaders

Ed Smylie was a leader at one of those pinnacle moments when his mastery of two pivotal leadership characteristics saved three men – and one nation's space program. The lessons for us as leaders two generations later are just as fresh as they were in 1970.

The first leadership characteristic Ed showcased was incredible resourcefulness.

We talk today almost casually about "thinking outside the box," but what does that really mean? Why is that important?

Creativity as leaders does not mean wild, crazy and unfocused actions that defy established boundaries; it means just the opposite – sane, innovative actions with a laser-tight focus on an objective that will redefine existing boundaries.

Resourcefulness is looking at what you have in new ways in order to accomplish important goals; it's creating clear, intelligent communication to convey those big-change ideas so that they are understood and valued by those who will implement them even under stressful circumstances.

Resourcefulness is not waiting for breakthrough technologies or a bigger budget or more oars in the boat to solve something that threatens the organization today; it's about using what you have with who you have when you have it to do what must be done now.

Resourceful leaders know the square peg can fit in the round hole if the stakes are high enough.

Would your team describe you as "resourceful"?

The second leadership characteristic Ed Smylie brought was a sense of calm. Yes, calm. This was a leader who knew the anxious captain loses the crew's focus and diminishes their potential at a time when only everyone's best can save the day.

Pressure is good; fear is not.

The situation demanded a cool, calm and supremely confident presence working methodically with his team to do what they did best – solve a difficult problem. At times of crisis, a team feeds emotionally off their leader. Leaders set the tone for greatness (or failure) often in a glance or a mannerism or in what they say and how they say it. When the team believes in the leader, there is nothing that cannot be accomplished.

What are you doing to inspire that kind of confidence? Be the leader that people want in charge when it matters most!

Things don't go wrong
and break your heart
so you can be bitter
and give up.
They happen to
break you down
and build you up
so you can be
all that you were
intended to be.

Samuel Johnson

Insight 9: Luck on the Horizon

Standing outside the Lucky Street YMCA in downtown Atlanta with a pillowcase, one change of clothes and not one penny in his pocket, Bob Williamson felt anything but lucky. The 24-year-old had just been released from prison in New Orleans for possession of heroin and had spent seven years hitchhiking across the country sleeping in ditches, shooting up drugs and living with one foot in the grave.

But deep inside this runaway was a desire to change – to be something more than the failure he had become. And change he would. From a job working with winos and addicts cleaning bricks for $15 a day, Bob Williamson would rise to become CEO of a $30 million software company and a nationally respected business leader.

But it happened by accident – literally.

Shortly after arriving in Atlanta, Williamson was in a head-on collision that sent him to the hospital for months. In that period of prolonged recovery, the young man saw his life with disturbing clarity and vowed to turn it around. It was a personal catharsis that found him discovering a deep sense of faith and a driving motivation to make something of his life – a revelation that set him on a path to incredible success.

Once recovered from his injuries, Williamson found a job with The Glidden Company, working in the company's basement putting labels on paint cans. It wasn't much but he made it noteworthy by doing more than was required in cleaning and organizing the area. His work ethic – first one there, last to leave – impressed his superiors who promoted him eight times in two years including a stint helping the company move to its first computer system. Bob went on to work for two other paint companies and became an expert in paint formulas.

It was an expertise he put to use in his basement for his own hobby as an airbrush artist. "I borrowed $1,000 on my Visa card and bought a bunch of chemicals and made a bunch of paint," he says. On a whim, he took his specialized paint to a trade show and became an almost overnight success. Excited, he quit his job and started his own paint company, Master Paint Systems, in 1977.

His business took off, and as it grew he hired programmers and began writing software for the company's warehouse, inventory control and supply-chain management. By 1986, his company was selling 6,000 art supply items and preparing to go public. But again adversity barred his path.

A pre-IPO audit uncovered that an accountant had embezzled the company to the brink of bankruptcy. Devastated but determined, Williamson fought through the setback, held off bankruptcy and grew the business back beyond even its previous levels. He eventually sold a healthy company and turned his entrepreneurial eyes on a new venture – software.

In 1992, Bob Williamson founded Horizon Software International. The company was built on the back-office software Williamson had spent years developing for his previous business. He adapted the systems to different markets but found a niche serving food distribution to school cafeterias. Horizon won the contract for the Los Angeles public schools, the nation's second-largest system and expanded into other institutions like hospitals, nursing homes, colleges and military bases.

Far removed from the destitute addict who arrived at the YMCA, Williamson, now in his sixties, has been married for more than forty years, has three children and presides over Horizon's 44,000-square-foot headquarters in downtown Atlanta.

Horizon employs more than 180 people and had $26 million in revenue in 2007. Deloitte honored it as one of the fastest-growing privately held companies in the United States four years running. Williamson won Business Person of the Year in 2006 in Gwinnet County, the third-largest Chamber of Commerce in the United States, and was also selected as a finalist for the prestigious Ernst and Young Entrepreneur of the Year event in 2008, an award whose alumni include such premier entrepreneurs as Michael Dell of Dell Computers and Arthur Blank, co-founder of The Home Depot.

Through it all, his business philosophy has not changed. Williamson says, "I'm the first one there and the last one to leave." The tone he sets as chief executive is value-driven. "I've always tried to be honest and straightforward, and not lie and not cheat, and not try to take an easy way out."

Bob Williamson keeps his success in perspective. "I'd been through so much in my life, I don't get discouraged," he says. "The trials I've had in business are mild compared to what my life was like."

Lessons For Leaders

Bob Williamson's story is an example of heroic inner growth.

His rise out of life's cellar to the highest levels of business and personal success reminds us of the potential we all have to excel when we leave yesterday's nightmares behind.

But before we can be leaders of others, we must lead ourselves. Before we can set the bar for others, we must set our own expectations. Before we can inspire others to reach for the brass ring, we must grab it first. Leadership of others begins with leadership of self.

There is no single recipe for personal leadership, but three key ingredients to any inner mastery must include declaration, discipline and determination.

To excel from within, we must change from within – we must declare to ourselves the change we desire. The act of declaration sets the goal in our mind and in our subconscience – like programming your mental GPS with the desired destination, giving your actions purpose, direction and a way to measure progress.

Then we must have the discipline to go where our goals lead us.

If we have set our sights sufficiently high, there will be challenge and adversity that demand a disciplined approach. Gandhi stated, "Be the change you desire to see in the world." We can adapt that to our own internal quest by being the change we want to see in ourselves.

Change demands discipline; it sets stringent standards, insists on stretching our goals (at times beyond our view) and evaluating our effectiveness with brutal honesty. But this is the fuel of self-leadership; discipline drives the engine of excellence.

Finally, at the core of leading ourselves is determination.

The road to success is littered with the broken dreams of the uncommitted.

Determination is the internal force to push through adversity, the willingness (almost eagerness) to beat even impossible odds and a dogged persistence that sees setback as a pothole in the road, not the end of the line. It is often the leader's refusal to quit or accept defeat that spurs others to raise their own game.

Bob Williamson had all three of these qualities – he declared his desire to change, he demonstrated the discipline to make changes and he was relentless in his determination to reach his goals. He followed the extreme path that illuminates the heights to which we can soar when we free ourselves of doubt, fear and regret and discover the hero that waits inside each of us.

He conquers who endures.

Persius

Insight 10: A Father's Eyes

A teenager lived alone with his father, and the two of them had a very special relationship. Even though the son was always on the bench, his father was always in the stands cheering. He never missed a game.

This young boy was still the smallest of his class when he entered high school. His father continued to encourage him but also made it very clear that he did not have to play football if he didn't want to. Yet the young man loved football and decided to hang in there. He was determined to try his best at every practice and perhaps he'd get to play when he became a senior.

All through high school the boy never missed a practice or a game, but remained a bench warmer all four years. His faithful father was always in the stands, always with words of encouragement for him.

When the young man went to college, he decided to try out for the football team as a "walk-on." Everyone was sure he could never make the cut, but he did. The coach admitted that he kept him on the roster because he always puts his heart and soul into every practice and, at the same time, provided the other members with the spirit and hustle they badly needed.

The news that he had survived the cut thrilled him and the first one he wanted to share the news with was his father, who immediately got season tickets.

This dedicated young athlete never missed practice during his four years at college, but still he never got to play in a game.

It was the end of his senior football season, and as he trotted onto the practice field shortly before the big playoff game, the coach met him with a telegram.

The young man read the telegram and became deathly silent. Swallowing hard, he mumbled to the coach, "My father died this morning. Will it be all right if I miss practice today?" The coach put his arm gently around his shoulder, "Take the rest of the week off, son, including the game."

Saturday arrived and the game was not going well. In the third quarter, when the team was ten points behind, a young man quietly slipped into the empty locker room and put on his football gear.

As he ran onto the sidelines, the coach and his players were astounded to see their faithful teammate.

"Coach, please let me play. I've just got to play today," said the young man.

The coach pretended not to hear him. There was no way he could take a chance in this close playoff game. However, the young man persisted and, finally, feeling sorry for the kid, the coach gave in.

"All right, go in," he said. What happened next stunned everyone. This unknown kid who had never played before was playing like a superstar.

The opposing team could not stop him. He ran, blocked and tackled like a star. His team began to triumph. In the closing seconds of the game, the kid intercepted a pass for the winning touchdown. His teammates hoisted him onto their shoulders. Such cheering you've never heard!

Finally, after the stands had emptied and the team had left the locker room, the coach noticed that the young man was sitting quietly in the corner all alone.

The coach came to him and said, "Kid, I can't believe it. You were fantastic! Tell me what got into you? How did you manage to play like that?"

He looked at the coach, with tears in his eyes, and said, "Well, you knew my dad died, and you knew he came to every game, but did you know that my dad was blind?"

The coach shook his head slowly in disbelief.

The young man swallowed hard and forced a smile, "Dad never missed one of my games in all these years, but today was the first time he could see me play."

*Author unknown

What we see in our mind's eye is far superior to what we see with our own eyes.

The father went to every game for his son because he knew that one day the success that was already in his son would have a chance to shine. The father did not need his eyes to see the greatness that lay within his son. He saw the young man's potential, so he reaffirmed that inner hero with his consistent attendance.

The father's presence was the son's inspiration.

Absence is not a reward for excellence. As a leadership trainer, I cannot count the times that I have counseled professionals to spend time with their best team members. Too often, leaders develop the mistaken notion that their strongest players are the ones they don't need to spend time with; they don't need to attend their functions or workplace.

Nothing could be farther from the leadership truth. When leaders spend time with their high-performing or high-potential team members, it signals their support and motivates their continued growth.

Time is one of the most precious commodities we can offer, so when we spend time with another person we acknowledge their value and reward their effort. We do not need an agenda or an action plan or a punch-list for time spent with our top performers; our presence is simply enough.

They will take that motivation and run with it.

The patience and persistence of the son also holds insight for us as leaders. For years, the son worked diligently toward a goal of playing in a game. He did everything that was asked, prepared himself and supported his teammates. Season after season, he kept his dream alive.

We often praise the action quality of leadership but we can miss the value of stalwart patience, the power in preparation, the significance of calm. But patience does not mean hibernation. Being vigilant for opportunity does not preclude making one when the time demands it. The son's persistence in gaining playing time after his father's passing is the result of his confidence spilling over into the moment – an unstoppable desire to excel when it mattered most. That's a quality all leaders share – the ability to not be denied when a critical window of opportunity opens.

Leadership isn't about how many minutes we play but rather what we do when we get our chance. It isn't about whether you're in the headlines or on the sidelines; it's about being ready on the frontline when it matters.

Leadership is supporting what we can't see but that we know is there. It's about helping others see the hero inside each of them. Leaders don't reward people with their absence; they inspire them with their presence.

Leaders have the courage to see the greatness in everyone. In the end, the son didn't become a star because his father died; the son was already a star because of how his father lived.

Strength does not come from
physical capacity.
It comes from
an indomitable will.

Mahatma Ghandi

Insight 11: No Bridge Too Far

It was probably one of the most spectacular father-and-son projects ever attempted. John Roebling and his son Washington were both talented engineers. The elder was the grand visionary who could see greatness where others saw only failure, while the younger was the pragmatist who could problem-solve any mechanical challenge.

It was 1870, and John envisioned a bridge connecting two urban hubs separated by one impossible body of water. Every expert of the time said it could not be done. It would be foolhardy to even attempt such a construction. They thought the elder Roebling mad.

At first, even the son was not convinced, but the father persisted and eventually the vision of this bridge took hold in the younger Roebling. He could see his father's dream, and so together the two hired a crew and began to build the bridge no one thought could be built.

The project started strong and each day the two grew more confident in their dream. They worked side by side and slowly the span took shape. But just a few months into the project, tragedy struck – a terrible accident claimed John's life.

But the son was not defeated and persisted in their work. Tragically, he too suffered a calamity that left him unable to walk, talk or move more than a single finger. It seemed all was lost.

Critics said it proved the bridge could not be built but Washington Roebling was not done yet.

His body was broken but the young engineer's mind was still sharp and keen, and he knew he could direct the work if only he could find a way to communicate. The only motion he had was movement in one finger and so he began tapping on his wife's arm as she sat next to him.

Together they worked out a code for communicating. He tapped and she translated his words to the engineers. It was painstakingly slow, but amazingly the project resumed.

For thirteen years, he tapped out instructions on his wife's arm and she relayed those to the engineers working on the bridge – thirteen years building a bridge he could not walk across. Thirteen years finishing a dream one tap at a time.

Today, the Brooklyn Bridge spans nearly 1,600 feet across the East River connecting Manhattan and Brooklyn and is still considered one of the masterpieces of engineering construction. It was the first steel-wire suspension bridge in the world and the world's longest suspension bridge for nearly thirty years after its completion. The Brooklyn Bridge carries millions of people a year and few, if any, know that it was built by a father with extraordinary vision and a son with an indomitable will.

Get the job done. If the bridge is not built yet, then we are not finished.

This is a remarkable story on so many levels. The first is in the power to envision grand achievement when every voice around you says you are crazy. John Roebling knew he could do something no one else had ever done and that everyone else said could not be built. But he not only saw the bridge; he shared that vision with his son Washington. And Washington bought into the dream. He believed in what his father was trying to do and he became so committed to the vision that he would let no amount of tragedy or outside pessimism prevent him from completing the objective.

How many of us are that committed to what we do? How many of us as leaders buy in to the goals of our organization or team with passion and energy? It takes undaunted, unrelenting commitment to get the job done. It takes courage to make someone else's dream your own and then press ahead through all manner of adversity to see it completed.

This story also reveals the incredible power of the human spirit. Reduced in body to movement of a single finger, Washington Roebling used what he did have in a keen mind and resilient spirit to accomplish what no one thought possible. What are we not finishing in our lives because we feel handicapped or limited? What are we overlooking in our own inner strength that can help us push through change, challenge or crisis? There is a hero inside each of us waiting to be discovered and unleashed.

Find a way to get the job done. Use what you have; don't lament what you don't. There are no bridges-too-far when the destination is your dream.

As with the migrant birds,
so surely with us,
there is a voice within,
if only we would listen to it,
that tells us so certainly
when to go forth
into the unknown.

Elisabeth Kubler-Ross

Insight 12: Geese and Chocolate

August 10 is never an easy date in my life.

On that date in 1998 my wife, Cynthia, finished her workday and was driving home, seven months pregnant and joyful about life. She never made it. A man high on drugs, and out to sell his poison, ran a stop sign at high speed and killed her and the baby.

The tragedy devastated my life and Ryan's life, our nine-year-old son. But for me, every day since then has been focused on carrying him through that nightmare and helping him discover the hero I know he has inside.

But I believe that journey may have finally ended.

On July 10, 2010, at the age of 21 and heading into his senior year at Syracuse University, Ryan bought an iconic chocolate business that was older than he was. Chocolate Pizza Company (*www.ChocolatePizza.com*) has been featured nationally on Food Network and ABC News and has an unbelievable gourmet chocolate line-up that serves thousands of retail customers and hundreds of businesses annually.

At one time, the store was across the street from our house. Cynthia used to take Ryan into the store in a stroller. The owner, Bonnie Hanyak, said she would watch as his little hand came up above the counter searching for the sample tray of chocolates. If he found it, his hand would quickly disappear with the chocolate treasure only to reappear moments later.

When he was fifteen and looking for his first job, Ryan asked Bonnie if she needed help. She didn't but she hired him anyway.

She was a wonderful boss for him to learn from – patient, hard-working, creative and successful. He worked at the store on weekends, school breaks and summers and whenever his schedule allowed.

He loved it, and less than a year later he told Bonnie that when she was ready to retire he was ready to own her business. Five years later, he did just that.

The toddler in the stroller is now a leader; the boy who dreamed of owning a company is now a man running one.

Ryan is responsible for a two decades-old business with employees who count on his judgment to maintain their jobs. He negotiates contracts, shapes marketing plans, manages inventory, handles customers, creates new products, invests in new equipment and leads a team that looks to him for motivation. He is in total command of every facet of his business.

I have quietly watched him assume all these responsibilities. I have worked with him in the store day in and day out, taking his direction and only occasionally adding my own opinion.

People ask me what it is like to work for my son, and I respond without hesitation that it is the best job I have ever had. I am part of my son's life in a way that would be the envy of most dads. My biggest challenge is to stay out of his way, to let him steer the ship and be there for counsel when he asks.

I have coached and mentored leaders all my professional life; it is what I do for a living, and while I am infinitely biased I know this to be true as a leadership coach: Ryan is good. He will be great. He has the tools. He has the heart. There are no limits on what he can achieve and who he can become.

I told all this to Cynthia on my trip to the cemetery on the 12th anniversary of her death. As I stepped out of the car and walked to her headstone, a flock of more than twenty Canadian geese came from nowhere and soared not fifty feet overhead, honking and flapping in that classic "V" formation.

I had to smile because they were flying west. She never could tell directions.

We don't see many geese in New York in August – in fact, I can't ever remember seeing them in the summer or flying west for that matter, but I took it as a good omen. Cynthia was watching and she was proud of her son.

That made two of us.

Scientists who study these things say that Canadian geese fly in a "V" formation because aside from the lead goose, the other birds find it 17% easier to move forward in that configuration. By drafting in the wake of the bird in front of them, the geese save energy and travel farther than if they were flying solo.

The honking, science says, is actually encouragement for the lead goose, a way for the team to urge the bird at the point to keep at it and draw strength from the flock. As the lead bird tires, another takes its place, and the aerial dance continues over thousands of miles to destinations unseen.

Ryan's entrepreneurial move reflects at least two leadership truths. The first is leaders set challenging goals and reach them.

They are not afraid to be bold in their thinking and bolder in their actions. Ryan knew at sixteen that he wanted to own Chocolate Pizza Company. He told people that and then he worked hard for years to put himself in a position to make it happen. Leaders live by a *carpe diem* philosophy. Do it now. Work for what you want. No one should want your dream more. As coach Paul Woodside says, "Big dreams should never come easy."

The second leadership truth is that effective leaders communicate a clear, vibrant vision for success.

Chocolate Pizza Company was successful before Ryan bought it but it had not scratched its potential. He could see that potential and laid out a vision for growth that has been his blueprint for taking the company to another level.

In his first two years as owner, Ryan grew sales 188% to over $800,000 a year. He opened a second location, increased Internet sales by 800% and now wholesales product at 350 locations in thirty-five states. He took a good company and made it great.

His leadership has been transformational for the business and reinforces the fact that vision is a verb not a noun.

Vision takes a dream, adds an action plan, motivates a team and then refuses to quit. I have listened to Ryan share his vision of growth with his employees, some of whom are more than twice his age. As leaders, we must find an entrepreneurial spirit that encourages us to take intelligent risks and invest ourselves fully in the task. Leaders draw from life experiences – maturity is not an age; it's a mindset.

I watch Ryan at work practicing the art of leadership and marvel at how unafraid he is, how decisive he is and how passionate he is.

He has things to learn, and some will not be easy or pleasant, but no steel is forged without flame and hammer.

Strength is only measured when it is tested so leaders never fear the struggle to be excellent. Ryan knows what true adversity is and lived through a nightmare that would have crushed lesser souls and yet he emerged hopeful, optimistic, energetic and confident.

Business will test him, but it cannot break him. He has already weathered far, far worse storms.

There were tears this day in the cemetery. The years have not changed that reality, nor should they. But amid the cascade of sadness over the absence of those we love were drops of joy over the presence of those we still have.

In the "Conquering Adversity" keynotes that I do across the country, I teach others to count blessings, not tears; life is full of both – but this time I took that lesson for myself.

Since that terrible day when I had to tell Ryan the unbearable news about his mom, I have felt like the lead goose, facing the headwinds, trying to carve a path through the air that would somehow make his journey easier, somehow help him reach a destination that even I could not see.

My place was always at the point. That is, until now.

I think I know why Providence brought geese overhead this evening. They were there to remind me that the point has a new leader. They were there to show me that I can drop back into formation now and simply encourage Ryan to move forward in his bold, new direction.

The boy is now a man and the man is now a leader.

The geese were there to salute a new leader and relieve an old (but very proud) one.

Closing Thoughts

"I finished *Inspired to Lead* over lunch one day because I couldn't put it down," said a friend of mine, referring to my previous book that also has twelve inspirational stories and leadership lessons. My friend told me that after reading the book, he ordered copies for each of his six direct reports. When the books arrived, he assigned each person two stories from the book. He told them to read the entire book but focus on the stories he had assigned them and connect those to the group's work. My friend said for the next twelve weeks he started each staff meeting with a discussion about one of the stories, led by the person assigned that one. What transpired, he said, was beyond his expectations, a process that everyone enjoyed and talked about all week. He said their conversations were open, candid and robust but really on-point. It was the best team building project they had ever done. But it got better. A few weeks later, his team, acting on their own initiative, repeated that process with each of their direct reports. He said he marveled at how something so simple could work so well. I told him there was nothing simple about inspiring a team, but that it always starts with a leader bold enough to lead by example.

The best leaders see opportunity for success in the most ordinary moments. They do so not just by recognizing the moment but by acting on it. My friend was inspired by the book he read but he saw the experience as more than that; he saw it as a platform to develop his team. And that team acted with their team. Leadership multiplied is at the core of extraordinary success.

Inform people and they will work hard. Inspire them and they will move mountains. Inspiration is not cheerleading, blind advocacy or insincerity. It does not make the challenge less formidable. It is not about feeling; it's about doing. But inspiration matters. It matters because there comes a point in the struggle when the difference between extraordinary success and epic failure is hearing a voice inside you that says, "Rise up, push on and get it done."

Meet the Author

Christopher Novak is an author, professional speaker and leadership coach whose rare combination of experience, empathy and energy make him a sought-after speaker and trainer. As a keynote presenter, he has inspired thousands of people nationally and internationally with his riveting "Conquering Adversity" message. Based on his book, this powerful, true-life presentation focuses on the hero inside each of us and what it takes to rise above change, challenge and adversity in our professional and personal lives.

To bring Christopher Novak to your next event, please contact him at:
E-mail: cnovak@twcny.rr.com
Website: www.ConqueringAdversity-speaker.com

WALKTHETALK.COM The Publisher
Resources for Personal and Professional Success

For over 30 years, WalkTheTalk.com has been dedicated to one simple goal…one single mission: To provide you and your organization with high-impact resources for your personal and professional success.

Walk The Talk resources are designed to:
• Develop your skills and confidence
• Inspire your team
• Create customer enthusiasm
• Build leadership skills
• Stretch your mind
• Handle tough "people problems"
• Develop a culture of respect and responsibility